# *The 7 Sense*

– MATTHEW WILSON –

FASTPRINT PUBLISHING
PETERBOROUGH, ENGLAND

www.fast-print.net/store.php

The 7 Sense



ISBN 978-184426-891-7

First published 2010 by
FASTPRINT PUBLISHING
Peterborough, England.

An environmentally friendly book printed and bound in England by
www.printondemand-worldwide.com

This book is made entirely of chain-of-custody materials

# *Dedication*

I dedicate this book first of all to my wife Barbara, who stood by me through thick and thin and never complained at me over the years, even when I became an RMN, through lonely times she gave me strength and I am proud to be her husband- Not forgetting our son mark who was Traumatized, hit over the head, now suffers from Brain Damage Anoxic diffused Cerebral brain damage I would also wish to thank my sons and daughter who gave me inspiration when I'm down last but not least I am proud of my mother who also from time to time gave me strength and encouragement in those early days may God bless them -

*Matthew*

# *The opening of the 7 sense*

What is meant by the 7 sense and what happens when you open this channel - we know and understand the 5 physical senses, also the 6 sense, but in essence the seven sense takes into account those abstract mental ideas waiting to be identified in the material world and manifest into verbal meanings the mind interprets. The mind is consolidator between that which is now and that which has to come the realisation becomes apparent when the third eye is opened within the circumference of its parts. . This pulsating energy is released by certain and positive commands to subconscious mind. When applied with determination and belief in its validity. The stream of energy coming from the soul finds its way through unimpeded gaining momentum and direction on its release into the ether. In the depths of my soul there is a light shining brightly bringing forth a continuous ray of hope and understanding giving me the strength to realise this powerful all embracing entity that knows no evil, and in the process purifying the material body, this thread of golden light awakens through continuous meditation which enriches and gives vitality to all sensations and material substance within the human body. When a man becomes soul infused he knows the fundamentals involved creating harmony. It as been suggested in some school of thought the soul is the all embracing fire that never goes out. But continues to burn adlib, these are just a few ways of expressing this powerful commodity, there are many other names given to identifying the soul. So now we know what the soul is and what it represents and presumably where it is situated within the body. The reason for this gives the reader some idea concerning the principals involved. The mind the brain and soul vibrate in unison and creates a continuous stream of an awareness. In the mind becomes the focal point and instigator from now on. The mind brings forward and now selects and distinguishes the thoughts to be carried into words and speech.

As I sit writing this manuscript I sense a host of people all sat in front of me, some smiling talking a few not doing anything . I see these people through my third eye. After a while they disappear as though they had never been there. Like puffs of smoke- each day these people appear to me and I now realise they are lost souls waiting to be recovered to their rightful abode. Decided to contact the spirit- undertakers so called whose job it is to take them to their respective places. There are thousands of lost souls floating around in the ether not knowing where they are and some don't realised they have past over into the spiritual realms. These are the ones who attach themselves to anyone who appears to be sensitive. This maybe why some people feel a presence around themselves but cannot communicate with these entities.

There as always been false prophets doomsday characters who have predicted disasters of a negative attitude. From burning buildings rail crashes - air disasters and so on there have also been religious fanatics who bless you with one hand and curse you with the other if you don't believe in what they teach. They use the power of thought and they don't realise the law of magnetic attraction - the saying is if you don't believe you will end up in hell and will be judged when your time is up, there is good and bad in all walks of life, some people are easily led and some having strong character, due to lack of understanding and knowledge these people are like lost sheep, they need guidance and motivation in their lives. Otherwise will not advance in their makeup and become static in most things they achieve. In most cases they say why can't I achieve the good things in life? Reason because they don't put anything into life but expect to get something out. It may take many life times for then to advance and purify their bodies for the soul to function through the mind unimpeded. Eventually everyone will progress and advance somewhat, for this is the path to a higher reality having this understanding you become soul infused.

This book is not for the faint hearted, a compilation spanning 70 years working in the field a most difficult one trying to unravel the mysteries that surrounds us all in this life. Many doubts and prejudice in the way of stumbling blocks and to be overcome even to begin with, I do hope we can all learn and contribute together some information that may help to illuminate false acquisitions and statements surrounding this phenomena in a way whereby we may all benefit at some stage in our search for the universal mysteries - this book is one of a kind, and gives a good account of its authenticity, and will inspire the reader to gain insight into this vast subject dealing with his own enquiry into the possibility of life after death. - first edition have a good journey matthew wilson 26/may 2010 as I sit writing this manuscript I sense a host of people all sat in front of me, some smiling talking a few not doing anything . I see these people through my third eye. After a while they disappear as though they had never been there. Like puffs of smoke- each day these people appear to me and I now realise they are lost souls waiting to be recovered to their rightful abode. Decided to contact the spirit- undertakers so called whose job it is to take them to their respective places. there are thousands of lost souls floating around in the ether not knowing where they are and some don't realised they have past over into the spiritual realms. These are the ones who attach themselves to anyone who appears to be sensitive. This maybe why some people feel a presence around themselves but cannot communicate with these entities. There as always been false prophets doomsday characters who have predicted disasters of a negative attitude. From burning buildings rail crashes - air disasters and so on there have also been religious fanatics who bless you with one hand and curse you with the other if you don't believe in what they teach. They use the power of thought and they don't realise the law of magnetic attraction - the saying is if you don't believe you will end up in hell and will be judged when your time is up, there is good and bad in all walks of life, some people are easily led and some having strong character, due to lack of understanding and knowledge these people are like lost sheep, they need guidance and motivation in their lives. Otherwise will not advance in their makeup and become static in most things they achieve. In most cases they say why can't I achieve the good things in life? Reason because they don't put anything into life but expect to get something out. it may take many life times for then to advance and purify their bodies for the soul to function through the mind unimpeded. Eventually everyone will progress and advance somewhat, for this is the path to a higher reality having this understanding you become soul infused.

Having insight and clairvoyance. This I believe strongly influence my life in so many ways, also knowing my spiritual guide white feather who over the years gave me inspiration and the ability to use and direct my mind purposefully - the times I said I would stop doing this type of work only to find I was doing more. To be amongst people and knowing for a fact that I could read their minds at times was little disturbing, so I had to close my psychic faculty down so as not to be attacked by other peoples negative thought which I picked up automatically. There were times when I thought for a moment I was going round the bend, but soon recognised these thoughts came from other people as well as spiritual ones. this is where the advantage of being a registered mental nurses training became an advantage knowing and studying the pathological and disturbed mind, this then was the answer to the previous problem, knowing the real from the unreal, in my book called the psychic nurse I have try to explain the difficulty was being a medium and also a psychiatric nurse at the same time. No matter how educated or clever you are you can still be afflicted with a mental problem. Which may effect you life in more ways than one.

Knowing the unreal from the real. How can we know this and what purpose can we derive from it. The mind is intricate mechanism where lies the answers to the many questions we want to bring into our lives unimpeded, through the understanding of the conscious and sub conscious mind comes the way forward that will give us the means to higher planes of existence and the knowledge we have access to bringing the two worlds together, the purpose is to develop a mind that can transcend time and space. Then the person becomes intuitive and relays information to his fellowman when required. Having said this the mind through constant training become the instrument whereby the real and unreal can be know. The stumbling blocks will no longer exist the thoughts will be of clarity and precise giving the person equilibrium in most things in his lie. The message now is loud and clear still the mind if possible through constant meditation and then it becomes a channel for truths. The question now arises why do we have to go and do all this to achieve eternal bliss, there is an answer somewhere in this sentence, well the magic is already there waiting for you to tap into. The mind then become a duel purpose entity and distinguished sources of information is available instantly. What do I mean by the 7 sense, we all have heard about the six sense and what it represents to those who possess it. In reality it is another plane of existence , which is used by a very few people into days world, many reasons come to mind . Suggested raised our thoughts to higher plane whereby the mind is the coordinator and interprets information coming from the ether so my definition of the 7 sense the universal mind we partake of but not aware of the attributes it entails - there are many conceptions and definitions regarding who as this extra sense , and in some instances can it be acquired and learnt in most cases it is a part and parcel of your individual makeup , relating from previous incarnations and becoming more pronounced in this particular life style so therefore it is an inbuilt mechanism within you through cultivation become an extension of the normal mind as we understand it to be. I have only begun to scratch the surface when trying to explain the fundamental principals involved in this vast areas we call the unknown therefore I suggest before we reject it , have an open mind and at the same time analyses with in reason the highs and the lows , taking on board the knowledge that there is to consume and digest on your journey into the unknown - written by matthew wilson to describe the indescribable to become an attractive force to be reckoned with on our stupendous journey we have taken on our path to enlightenment and at this stage things begin to happen after many years of malipulation, the mind develops an intriquite way of dealing with the rubbish that as accumulated within this all pervading entity sorting the wheat out from the chaff, there are many modes of expressive thought developing within the active mind at this stage the stillness of the waters overflowing with reasurrence now help the inner mind of lower one if you prefer this way of describing it with an abundance of solidifying substance as you my now say all the above is just rhetoric and maybe meaningless to many , therefore read dijest and recall that which maybe of benefit to you at this particular time. There is so much I can give and there is so much you can take aboard. I feel I have now taken a modest methodical approach giving you various constructive ways and means of analysing the essence and nature of the world beyond. My mother who passed away in the year 1994 always said I would do good work and she influences me from the spiritual world guiding me in the right direction and at the same time doesn't interfere with my life, we don't realise the love mothers give to their children we take it for granted. My mother belongs to a band of people who assist those who have past over but don't realise they have done so to help them through that transition which we all have eventually to go through. many people end up in darkness until they are taken by the hand to their respective places by those so called spiritual undertakers this may sound a little way out, but I believe this when I spoken by my mother to me. Her voice is just the same as when she was on the earth plane. And this goes for all those other entities who have by their distinguished voices, if you have the ability to be clairaudient, or better still have the power of clairvoyance been able to see them as they were upon the earth plane. looking at some photograph can give you certain characteristics of a person either past or alive, the impressions appear in your mind the problem then it to be able to interpret was you receive and give to whoever is at hand to receive them - it may be something rather small something about their personality and a way of life, most people when receiving messages from spirit think of the here and now is it happens, it might be to do with a condition a person had before passing over, this information is first of all to give prove of survival. Of life after death.

It gives me great pleasure to be able to come to your earth plane at this moment in time, I come with peace and harmony to one and all respectively of their creed and religion. I have listened with great care to what as been said by my channel Martello while writing this book, a wonderful synopsis if I may say so. I give him credit where it is due and know for fact his writings are authentic and illuminating, I know this to be true as I give him the information. The spirit world are looking for those who are aspiring and are prepared to take up the challenge in this day and age to commit themselves to spiritual beliefs. not many are prepared to take up the gauntlet and open the door of perception, I suppose it would not do for everyone to have the 7 sense, taking into account the lack of information regarding the spiritual planes of existence and the lack of experience in this mysterious field. Anyhow I come to your earth plane with love and peace and I want you all to be of good cheer and have faith in your beliefs. I know the time will come when decisions have to be taken do not be afraid spirit will guide you and give you strength when required. Hold your heads up high you have began your spiritual journey into the unknown, I have no fear as the lord above also guides you. Good look in everything you do. From white feather spirit guide.

The secret behind this illusive concept will open up vista of information never before recognised giving a broader sense of individualisation once the attraction through visualisation and imagination, the two keys elements needed for the mind to recognised the ability following the most advanced information coming through adlib. You are the intricate mechanism on this planet earth. No other species has the ability to change and transform the things around him, he as capacity to alter anything that is presented to him in his life. Because he knows the laws of attraction. Through this mode of expression he can also when required give a very good advise to his fellowman. what is the purpose behind all this, according to the teachings in metaphysical documentaries, we are evolving towards perfection in this cosmic jungle, maybe this is why there are differences between human beings all on different levels of evolution that give us the probable of distinction do we really know the cause of effect and the many misunderstandings it causes throughout our earthly lives or is there some other answer to this problem when we scrutinise in-depth the reason why we alter our minds instantly for better or worse, someday we may have the answer - the secret behind this illusive concept will open up vista of information never before recognised giving a broader sense of individualisation once the attraction through visualisation and imagination, the two keys elements needed for the mind to recognised the ability following the most advanced information coming through adlib. You are the intricate mechanism on this planet earth. No other species has the ability to change and transform the things around him, he as capacity to alter anything that is presented to him in his life. Because he knows the laws of attraction. Through this mode of expression he can also when required give a very good advise to his fellowman. what is the purpose behind all this, according to the teachings in metaphysical documentaries, we are evolving towards perfection in this cosmic jungle, maybe this is why there are differences between human beings all on different levels of evolution that give us the probable of distinction do we really know the cause of effect and the many misunderstandings it causes throughout our earthly lives or is there some other answer to this problem when we scrutinise in-depth the reason why we alter our minds instantly for better or worse, someday we may have the answer -

The realisation of the 7 sense gives you the wonderful understanding about people and their lives, knowing what is in your brothers heart at any given moment having dedicated ones life to this subject opens a new field of enquiry, into the relationships and the methods of obtaining spiritual truths. Far beyond earthly experiences, becoming a vehicle whereby hidden knowledge is brought to the mind of the seer to be past on to those seeking and searching for the divine thread which binds us all together so that we can become whole once gain in this universal concept we call spirit. Fortunately we can rectify the very of the lower self through the methods of introspection if and when we decide to follow our inner guidance each day through realising that outcome. Having mastered the art of meditation through certain rituals the mind then becomes the bearer of infinite solutions and can at ay given moment realise the quality of what is to be said, I can only give to you what I receive from spiritual mentors to be past on to those people having the privilege to be given messages from their loved ones through psychic channels whereby the information is founded upon the information know prior to the medium - the immediate response given when a psychic gives a message where did it come from? How can this come into manifestation without anyone knowing before hand the contents given by the medium. There are many questions to be answered if possible about this phenomena. The answer is that the medium psychic channels are opened then there is a three ways communication which takes place between the medium and his guide who is in contact with sitters loved ones. The mystery is what is the mechanism bringing this unique episode into manifestation, in there a magical formula ? There are different modes of expressions when this clairvoyant reality becomes apparent. All this is due to mediums ability to interpret what as been given to him or her, at that given moment. The mediums experience and motivation will decide what kind of message is been channelled - there is a point whereby the past is recognised in detail and the present as it is, then there is the future which has not arrive yet. may be given to the sitter - past - present - future in reality's all one it is human beings who separate this trio into that which as gone - that which is and that as not manifested called future.

The time getting nearest for you to realise your true potential the difficulty you may ask yourself at this time stage is will it work having listen to what as been said, you may now star to concentrate and meditate, by doing this you will engage into unknown. First of all you must be relaxed sitting in comfortable chair, then start to breath counting one to ten. This is to clear the mind and rest the brain also creating a vacuum so that all thoughts entering the mind become obsolete. You are now beyond your thoughts, you appear to be surrounded by peace and harmony you are relaxed from your head to your toes. what next you may ask, the next stage is for you to visualise yourself out of your physical body and see yourself sat in the chair this then proves the spirit is and can survive without the physical body. You are now in your astral body and can move and travel to places just by thinking this. You also can now see with the third eye. All this is termed altered states of consciousness. And can be brought on by drugs - anxieties - deprived or lack of oxygen - neuron chemicals trauma. The scientific world does not except certain altered states of mind as been genuine, rather like mental disorders. No foundation and at times classed as hallucination having no characteristics associated with delusions this is the psychiatric terminology ? The mediums work being a medium does not mean you will be rich, have a nice house knowing the lotto numbers winning the pools having the best of everything, not on your nelly. In fact the complete opposite in the real world. Everyone wants to know if they will win pools it is common factor with us human beings, clairvoyance cannot produce the goods you crave for, only outline if there is a possibility of you getting the things seen by the seer. And the timing can be short period of time or long time for the prediction to manifest the secret lies in the ether and what takes places is a thought is projected by the seer and eventually like magic projects the image on to the screen of the clairvoyant, this is when they say I see a brighter future it is just around the corner and will bring you money or success, never mind the tall dark stranger who nine times out of ten appears there and then in your clairvoyant reading. So in reality the medium first priority is to prove that life continues beyond the grave by contacting those who have past away into the afterlife. This is process that takes place, a good medium requires no objects to concentrate on just direct communication between the two world. To able to deliver information is wonderful thing. Like today's radio no wire attached, picking up the right station and tune in.

# *Fear of death*

The majority of people fear dying don't even want to talk about it for many reasons, (1) what will happen to me (2) where will I go (3) what will I do (4) how will I know I am dead ? (5) will I be different to what I am now (6) will I grow older (7) will I still have my pain and conditions (8) is the afterlife far away (9) do you drink and eat (10) will I see my relatives and loved ones the above questions are ask at times you will live without your body, and you will go to place you have made for yourself while on the earth plane. You will learn more lessons. You will know you are dead when you can look back at our body lying lifeless on the bed. The only difference will be your spiritual body. No there is no time in the afterlife - your physical pain you will no longer have. The afterlife is all around you here and now, no food or drink required, yes you will see your relatives and loved ones in fact they will come to you and help you with your transition to the next world. I hope I may have answered those sensitive questions people ask. About dying, there is no death.

This section of manuscript is about the demonstration of medium ship I carried out over the years I knew from an early age I had the gift of insight, but I thought everyone had this awareness. Even while at school I knew what other children were thinking and sometimes knew what they had in there packets my mother god bless her soul told me I would be a very good medium. My mother took me to spiritual church to do spiritual work I did not demonstrate my perception for a few years, I was gaining experience my mother was also a good medium and did demonstrations I remember going to see a client and I gave her prove of spirit by brining her dad through and gave her his name and his condition before passing to he higher side of life. She was over the moon and very pleased with this information, her dad told her to stop worrying about their so Michael who had just been in a car accident, but would recover - I felt warm sensation running through my body on this occasion , I knew then spirit was guiding me. There were many times people would get in contact with me saying that I had just seen their friend and would I go to see them. This came often by word of mouth. I was soon giving demonstrations in different towns on one particular time gave a demonstration in the winter gardens to full house. I remember I felt nervous given messages, and then a voice said to me you will be fine, I will not let you down. I knew then it was my guide telling me this, I then felt calm and relaxed - in between giving demonstration on large scale I gave readings, I remember the time I was invited to a large house on the Blackpool road the owner had seen me giving demonstrations and rang me to ask if I would be able to see at least 20 people and would I confirm this. This I did and told her it would not be for a week as I had others to see. I came up with an idea, I phoned a very good friend who also a good medium to join me in venture, he answered and said yes. On arriving at this residence to give reading I was surprised to find there were 30 people not 20. Somehow I must have known this to have my good friend accompany me. What we suggested was for him to do so many and then I would take over. This we did they were all seated waiting for us to commence. He went straight into a trance as he was trance medium it was revelation to hear what he came out with this lady on the front was amazed at what he told her he mentioned her sister and brother in spit when they were young, sister fell of a house and injured her spine and did not walk after that, he got a standing aversion from the rest of the crowd, the next person he brought through was a man in his sixties who suffered from heart failure and had diabetes on this occasion he transfigured his face changed to the person coming through. The next person he told she could not place what he had told her so he said take it with you also ask someone in family ok she said. Time flew by and by this time he had done 10 people and needed to recharge his batteries. I then stared to do my stint, and went to three ladies whom spirit told me were mother and two daughters and this spirit person said its your husband and father. To the two daughters, he went on to say how he used to grind his teeth and was sorry to hear his older daughter was upset losing a baby at birth , but did say the child was with him in spirit and at times comes close to you, he went on to say happy birthday dear wife - time was passing by me and we knew we could not go to everyone, so we decided to have a group session with the rest of the people this they agreed on and spirit came through to most pf the people who were left, my friend gave a demonstration of his transfiguration and the ability to communicate with spirit voice we then had a break as the room became hot with all these people and was given refreshments. We managed to communicate with a few more people and then gave some philosophy regarding the spirit world and the many planes of existence, overall it was a good meeting and it was said for us to come back in the near future, we said we would when the time was right. It can be very exhausting and energy loss when in that clairvoyant realty they could not get enough and said how enlightening it had been which was nice to hear.

I have written several book on the subject of the psychological journey to the spirit world my latest one is called the psychic nurse a true story about having the gift of second sight while working in a psychiatric hospital to study the pathological mind and the treatments used in this field of knowledge. First became interested due to the fact I was in Korea attached to the 26 field ambulance and when I got demobbed went from one job to an other and then decided to become a student nurse and did a three year course and passed my exam and then became a registered mental nurse. so you can imagine what it was like to nurse the mentally sick - somehow I was not troubled by any deceased entities who I saw frequently walking up and down the long green and white corridors - lots of patient whom I had look after thought they were still alive going about the hospital, some began to realise they had past over and realised this, you can imagine the dilemma I was in, hearing voices and seeing spirit wearing a white coat. I felt at ease within the surroundings of the hospital but many times I had to close my channels down otherwise would loose a certain amount of energy, this was at times very difficult to do. The training I did put me in good stead studying the pathological mind and the many inflictions that can occur with the mind. Not many people were prepared to do this kind of work. I suppose you must be cut out to do this job. It took me a while to get to know each patient by name this and the conditions they were suffering from . Friends and relatives would say to me, they could not do this type of work and I must be out of my mind no comment was given in answer to that question. The nurses soon found out about me and insight I had and nicknamed me thc psychic nurse. Those were happy days I spent working in a psychiatric hospital. You wont believe the next thing I am going to say, here goes I was given the task of taking patients who had passed away to the hospital morgue, they said I would be suited by this knowing what I was - on one particular occasion I was assisted with a student nurse to take a body to the freezer, and it was snowing, the patient as on a ward adjacent to the main hospital and we had to go outside to get there, so you could see the difficulty we had in those days, the porters didn't remove bodies in those days. So what happened we were pushing the trolley when it decided to get stuck in the snow and the patient rolled off the trolley that was not our lucky day. We managed to get the body back onto the trolley and made our way to the morgue. The student nurse was now nervous and said will he be ok now. I replied well he would not have felt a thing I feel a lot better now knowing what you are besides being a nurse, I don't feel scared any more. We arrived at the morgue and placed the body in the shute so called the made our way back to our prospective wards -

Do we realise the world we occupy is created by thought. You may say how is this, or better still can the mind project thought processes into the ether causing human beings to react to each other owing to interactions produced every time thought becomes words if we could see what takes place when this occurs. Would it be possible for the mind to create a way whereby negative conditions can be transferred into positive ones. Human beings have this unique potential built into their individuality which is called personality. Which we project to others at any given time. there is so much irresponsible rhetoric sent out into the cosmos, this is why we at any given time become irritable and in some cases depressed and lethargic in situations beyond our individual responses. When we take a closer look at this concept, we begin to notice this is feasible why we react like this to our fellowman. The above may sound a little way out, after taking into account the state of mans inability to respond to this probability, eventually fiction maybe fact in a world full of dissatisfaction. I hope through this we may become in tune with our fellowman creating harmony and peace. When we send out negative thoughts into the ether ewe are not aware of this dilemma, they maybe lots of people who will disagree with what I have suggested is only a thought.? When we have established a certain amount of knowledge coming from the soul we the realise the metaphysical structure within our selves and the meaning of life in all is profundities the many deep layers covering the existing soul eventually becomes a reality and the release of this idea produces a wave of energy never before envisage, this due to the realisation between spirit and matter. Soul will go on occupying material form over many of hundred of years. Each reincarnation brings into manifestation a new impetus if that is the right word to express a new beginning along side the old personality. To gather further experiences towards the souls unique equilibrium. According to the study of psychology this inherent psychological process goes into deep infinity then becoming an overwhelming concept beyond time and space. I better come down from the clouds, otherwise we will be in a situation whereby truth becomes fiction and vice versa. I hope this makes sense to the reader in my attempt to rediscover the alternating presumption within the bounds of probability that the soul continues beyond the gave. The picture becomes clearer with each reincarnation, you may now ask what is the purpose behind all this acquired knowledge we gather on our journey from the atom to the mot sophisticated human being upon this planet we call earth, Why do we call the soul sometimes the spirit, did the name arise from the Greek mythology and Greek terminology it as been suggested the soul in man synonymous with and is associated with spirit - personality - consciousness and sometimes the psyche. Taking into account all these different expressions relating to the terminology, the big question arises is it imagination or some ideology create my mans futile way of saying I am more than I appear to be in the cosmic sphere rotating in the universe. No one can claim without a shadow of a doubt its authenticity as a living concept. As we have said this notorious powerful energy pervading throughout the material body. They are many ways to try and tune in to this specific energy if possible bringing forth this eternal light also know as the spark of divinity - but been suggested for what purpose is there in all this are we any nearer to the origin from whence it was first recognised. maybe not owing to many diversities surrounding its originality, so do we take this as an expected situation now knowing, so do we take as an excepted situation now when there is the possibility it maybe so. Idea's hold the key when we take it for granted, there is without a doubt the soul continuation beyond the physical and material concepts we presume as life.

# *Psychic readings*

This part of my manuscript is about my experiences over the years giving and displaying medium ship in various locations when you have the gift of insight people who are interested phenomena will immediately make their way to see you for different reasons, some want their way to see you. Afterlife and contact their relatives and loved ones, while the appear to be more interested in mundane things and future aspects waiting around the corner the old saying is to be forewarned is to be forearmed, and there is a possibility that the future can be altered by avoiding certain pitfalls that arrive on our doorsteps if known ? The above is a brief description and an account of a mediums ability to convey information given by spiritual guides. To be passed on to those anticipation recollections of those loved ones who have departed from this earth. You may think I have been swinging phenomena I have tried as best as I can to illustrate the mechanisms and what takes place when in clairvoyant reality.

In the 1970s and 80s I attended a lot of psychic fairs with other practiceners exhibiting their various gifts and was surprised at the volume of people visiting these seminars, some just curious while others looking for god reader. I was asked on many occasion by some who is good I would I recommend them, this I refrained from answering, actually I said go to the one you are drawn to or attracted by. People were queuing up to have their cards read very few palmist to note, but plenty of mediums, being a rmn gave me better insight into people conditions plus my clairvoyance, at times the hall was pact and people going from one stall to an other seeing if thy came up with the same conditions. Those were the days when psychic were bubbling and did a roaring trade. One of the downsides was energy loss I found after awhile had to recuperate while card readers did not lose any. These are reasons I won't go in to at this stage. Knowing what people are thinking at times made people sit up and were surprised at this. My ability came naturally not force in any way. There were some people who did not understand at times what you were referring to and at this particular time could not place what was said as they were looking at the here and now. Many times I said ask someone in your family who will probably know the persons from the afterlife who have come through on your vibration. There were times when some did just that and were very pleased after querying what had been passed on and came and told me this.

# *Masonic hall*

I was asked by a masons if would do a demonstration in their Lincoln lodge I said I would. I phoned Peter who by the way lives in Nottingham not far away from Lincoln and asked him if he would do a demonstration in a Masonic lodge, yes was his answer. We were going to do Sat - and Sunday it was advertised in the Lincolnshire echo and tickets were available throughout local shops. Saturday night we had a packed hall it surprised me how many people were interested in these demonstrations. Peter was a transfiguration medium. we began by giving some philosophy and then stared to demonstrate clairvoyance there was men as well as woman - the atmosphere was electric, I began by going to a man on the second row whose vibes I picked up instantly - there is a lady in spirit who comes very close to you and is giving me the name Ann, he replied and said it was his mother who had past over just recently, also a lady called Lilly is now standing beside you sending you her love. That's my wife god bless her. I was the drawn to a lady sat about in the middle of room and gave her a lady who was blind and lost her sight in a car accident. Holding a wrist watch you gave her with elevated hands so she could tell the time her eyesight is now complete and can see clearly. I then went to the back of the room, I was drawn to a lady wearing red coat the a man appeared and held her hand showing me a ring he gave her for her birthday, and gave me the name Margaret I then sat down and let Peter take over.

# Peter going into a trance

So now it was Peters turn to demonstrate, the hall went deadly silent, you could hear a pin drop, the audience waited with baited breath not knowing what to expect, then Peter voice changed and started to speak, my name is John and I come to a lady on the third row, she recognised the name and the voice to let people know who he was this then got the crowd going and gave Peter a standing aversion. He then went to a young girl in her 20s and gave her the name marry, then once again the voice changed and said its your Nan, the young girl had tears in her eyes and then thanked Peter for his wonderful message. We then rough the meting to close what Peter does takes a lot of energy and felt he had lost some. It appeared that Peter heading for something maybe a vius, as it was he could not carry on, se we had to cancel the Sunday owing to his condition and told them would be back in the near future, the audience was pleased with what they saw. We could not say exactly when we would be back unknown to us they were reporters in the audience and did a write up the next day - Peter rang me an explaining that he was lot better and the doctor prescribed him some antibiotics for a chest infection. That goes to show you were are all human. you don't have to go far in this day and age before you come across someone who has the gift of insight, or the many books published about psychic phenomena. Its as been suggested people go to see psychic more times than seeing a doctor, why is this, because somehow a doctor asked you what's up what are you complaining about, he can see your signs but not your symptoms where as a psychic can see your symptoms at a glance and give you advice about it. With me been a psychic and a nurse I could diagnose what the person was suffering from. Where as you tell the doctor what your problem is then and then he prescribes medicine for your condition. Some people suggest you have X ray vision to be able to see their problems, that's one way of putting it, in respect a person should be treated with mind - body and spirit. As a whole person and not one particular area. There are many who do just that to help and speed up the persons immune system. This is the difference between a doctor and a good psychic to be able to meet someone in the street and an have no prior knowledge about them, then you tell them something which as meaning to them or their love ones from the other side is a wonderful gift, this as happened to me on many occasions as though spirit was wanting to give them a message. When this takes place the person sometimes says you wont believe this I was just thinking about that person in my mind. After dedication my life from being a child to the present day I realised the time was for me to put my experiences in a book about spirituality so that people could read for themselves the ups and downs being a practicing clairvoyant / medium.

There were times when you could take on board to many peoples conditions being an open vessel made you more susceptible to other peoples problems which they carried around them. My doorkeeper job was to filter through and at times reject incoming thoughts from those past over so that you become in command of all you survey when in that clairvoyant reality. As been suggested the main item was to bring into focus that there is no death, the first principal we were taught before anything else. Once this was established other items of a mundane character concerning everyday activities could be dispatched to the sitter, people still ask me how did I do it and why if I knew things before they happened, I was not rolling in money, knowing the outcome of event it as been said many times by different people that the gift of sight is not to become rich but to help people who need guidance in their lives. But as we all know there are those who make it a business telling the future event, this is not new, also I have been asked with some if I knew any good clairvoyant besides me. I then said a was not in a position to comment on that subject. I suppose this is natural wanting to know this, as there are good and bad in all professions, and so it went.

As I sit writing this synopsis I feel a presence very close to me giving me reassurance prompting me in writing this manuscript as I feel at times a voice whispering words for me to pass on their knowledge to those on the earth plane. This happens a lot with music and great musicians passing down songs and philosophers pouting literature to those who are aspiring to develop there talent back on the material plane, so communication does not stop when the body ceases to function the higher faculty opens up a new field of anticipation and enquiry into thought activity.

there are many spiritual guides giving reassurance to those who open their minds to this abstract phenomena when the time is right and certain steps taken upon the ladder metaphorically speaking a multitude of questions arise within the neophytes mind bringing a new sense of direction, in some instance testing the stability whereby a platform is erected and the sowing of seeds are planted firmly joining the antakarana the golden bridge to the world above and the world below. In my experiences I have over the years help people to come to terms with detrimental psychic episodes hindering their lives. Whereby they seek ways and means of closing down their channel to bock the incoming negative thoughts playing havoc upon the brain cells.

As child I saw spirit people and thought this was normal my mother who as past some 15 years ago was blessed with the gift if insight and was a very good clairvoyant in her day. Taught me many aspects of the spiritual world. As I got older I developed both clairvoyance and clairaudience and did platform working in churches which gave me more experience. I was reading all kinds of books on the mind and psychology which opened my channel more and gave me stability in the readings I gave. People world ring me ask me all sorts of questions ranging from am I going to win the pools what's going to win 230 at york races tomorrow . My spiritual experiences, but I suppose the time was not right. As I became older and did less consultations I decided to start writing down my experiences. this is just a brief account of my early experiences having now devoted my life to helping people to adjust in their lives

I have after many years of giving evidence concerning the after-life come to a conclusion that there is a world beyond the physical material one we live and have our being. Although the evidence for many loopholes in as much our perception is limited , the reality remains sufficient for further study without being premature in our outlook . It still remains a big mystery in our lives, especially when no one as yet come back into physical form, it is very interesting when evidence comes though from a person who as past over gives an account in detail of their experience while on the earth plane previous to them passing .where does this information come from? It certainly does not come from the practitioners head. Who is just acting as a channel whereby this information is past directly to sitter. So therefore it appears to be communication given to the medium via his spiritual guide who acts as a conduit between the living and so called dead. I cannot expand on this as we are not yet able to examine scientifically the proof of this abstract phenomena n a elaborate way - indeed been able to confront those irritating moments that appear to upset your everyday activity can be an advantage relieving built up tensions and set you on the road to becoming more reliable when confronted with obstinate questions that arise out of the blue, I am not saying we should analyse every detail when this comes into focus, but with a little bit of common sense you may come up with the right idea to deal with the situation instead of repressing the thought. Also the time will arrive you have to decide what you want to achieve studying the paranormal- words can means different things to different people at different times. Although the outcome maybe similar when first noticed there maybe discrepancies with the finer detail. On further analysis - I know how difficult it can be to give ones full attention when the mind becomes elevate to higher principals these interactions stable. I presume by now your taste buds become more active in this process of acquiring the knowledge and wisdom of the ancient wisdom opening this field of knowable concepts, I feel when the opportunity arise the process will become normal- memories and all experiences are locked deep within the soul and occasionally at times come to the surface effecting the conscious, making us happy or some instances feelings of depression, inadequate, making your lives for a moment dull and lethargic, this is one of the problems that effect us in our daily lives, in psychiatry these are sometimes called repressed ideas which become deep rooted in this subconscious concept. There are many aspects concerning this intricate mechanism and many different approaches associated with it to try and understand what it is that is causing the person to be at a low state of affairs. if we realise these impeding attributes give rise to personality disorders causing abnormal within the mind. In the majority of those who seek enlightenment this is overcome through sheer consistency while meditating closing the mind whereby thought becomes none existent- through the silence all things become manifest, his is one of the big mysteries we are confronted with when starting upon the spiritual ladder beginning our journey towards enlightenment in this particular round hope I have not strayed to much from the knowledge concerning the soul in manifestation. As there are numerous methods of realising the intricate ways of knowing the ultimate we need to examine different methods and approaches needed to even begin to become motivated towards peace and harmony that comes though the realisation we are spiritual orientated we all have the ability to transcend through the mind this all inspiring knowledge - Now we have come to a point in this elusive dynamic perception. Having now realised this incoming force, the mind relays the individual to point whereby a higher sequence becomes indispensable bringing the intuition nearer and within the range of the conscious mind. The psychic channels become more vibrant now that the way as developed into a two way system. Where have we been so far in unfolding and recognising this creative power, actually we have not moved an inch physically. But mentally the mind as travelled in many directions entering new episodes never before encountered. the interesting thing now, is it possible if we follow these instructions will we become a prognosticator the guardian of the hidden truths. Having now felt this attractive energy in the silence while meditating the soul illuminates the mind bringing the spiritual lights in accordance with the persons state he as reached in this round. never the less attitudes can prevent a person from being spiritually minded, because if the law of attraction applies the mind will only receive that which is projected in the first instance.

The secrets of the universe will unfold to the man who as aligned his mind and spirit and soul becomes active, this realisation comes about through concentration meditation-contemplating stilling the conscious mind creating a vacuum in space and time. When this occurs there is a definite awakening of the soul becoming activated through the material body. when the man acknowledges this incoming energy he becomes a channel whereby a constant stream of force engulfs the thoughts that enter the nard is in the etheric body- this attractive energy brings about a balance and stabilises the whole system, a direct action results in the recognition whereby understanding becomes a reality.

So far I have taken you from the material world into the spiritual domain and what have we found? On our journey, may I first say we have not travelled far in fact we have not moved from were we are. You have travelled in your minds eye, leaving your physical body, and in the process we are moving around and what do we find and see, nothing really different from the normal world. The only difference to note is that we don't need a material body. if for instance you want to go and see or contact someone all you have to do is think about it and you will be transported immediately, we move and travel by our very thoughts to where ever you may want to go . This is what you do when in the world beyond. This may take some digesting. When you have the gift to see beyond the physical senses you use this concept. the move we use this abstract mode of expression the more we become conversant with this other so called world. But in reality it is the same world without your material counterpart.

The immediate response given when a psychic gives a message, where did it come from? How can this come into manifestation without anymore knowing before hand the contents given by the medium. There are many questions to be answered if possible about this phenomena. The answer is that the mediums psychic channels are opened then there is a three way communication which takes place between the medium and his guide who is in contact with sitters loved ones. the mystery is what is the mechanism brining this unique episode into manifestation, is there a magical formula? There are different modes of expressions when this clairvoyant reality. Becomes apparent. All this is due to the mediums ability to interpret what as been given to him or her, at that given moment, the mediums experience and motivation will decide what kind of message is been channelled - there is a point whereby the past is recognised in detail and the present as it is, then there is the future which has not arrive yet. may be given to sitter-past-present-future in reality's all one it is human beings who separate this trio into that which as gone -that which is and that which as not manifested called future.

The passing of time is an automatic response and cannot be stopped although is suggested time is man made. Giving access to measure from one point to another but waits for no man regardless who he is or where he maybe. The length of time in the spiritual sense is none existence in the spirit world in just is. As soon as we start talking about time beyond the senses we can become confused in our way of thinking. the spirit world is in essence nothing but the thought world. So if you can imagine the spirit world is all around us here and now, but we tend to recognise subtle energy as such the mind can travel unimpeded seeing things and communicating with like minded people at distances and returning with information. Profiling- astral travelling are just names to identify this concept. There are many books giving instructions how to develop this metaphysical component in bookstores. Many have tried to develop this channel but without success and some have mastered the psychological principals. the man who takes each step one by one becomes more proficient developing and recognising the way forward into the realms of the divine, precipitation and anticipation brings about the quality needed within the spectrum. What makes a man decide the path he should take on this mysteries journey in his life, maybe he is not satisfied with what he has got, knowing for a fact there is this something bigger and more everlasting than the physical characteristics he is endowed with.

The psychological and philosophical approach concerning the illusive mind cannot be summed in a few words the study and continuity of thoughts entering at any given moment, can be assess with detail and analysis giving rise to acquired reason of contempary nature. Within the structure of any sequence of numerous attempts with possible effects arriving on the scene where thought can be rearranged in an order fashion bringing together added information to be verified as a continuous process. when the above becomes an attitude of mind, there is nothing to prevent a person becoming a master of the wisdom. In his life, he as become soul infused and a light bearer in the presence of his fellowman. He as overcome certain abnormalities and developed a strong attitude in his approach he is an inspiration to one and all, the perseverance and dedication as eventually paid dividends elevating the very essential method of approach methodically taken on the journey of discovery. the spiritual magnetic soul infused person as become independent from all adversities and can recognised as a solidified reliable person who can now give total commitment when ask to give to his fellowman, the foundation stone upon the mans existence was created from the very first time he arrived upon this planet in past incarnations, together the in this particular life. Accumulation in a specific manner as to become intriguingly an outstanding unique person. The quality of life depends on the direction we take towards our fellowman and the reason for our failure there are many solutions at our fingertips if we realised we are not isolated in this vast arena within the spectrum of understanding in this cosmic sphere. To begin with we must alter our attitudes if possible and give our fellowman the benefit of the doubt. we are the totality of all human existence on the planet earth. And we have the ability to transcend time and space through the direction of the mind. Expanded conscious ness becomes apparent when the soul becomes activated through continuous meditation, stilling the mind to a pint whereby nothing can enter to disturb the mind while in this state equilibrium the inner quality of the soul penetrates and vibrates the mind and body. the describe this phenomena in words is beyond reason the feeling of joy and peace becomes a normal sequence from now on changes in a positive nature arrives within the brain and mind, enlightening the way forward attracting and motivating the psychic doorways. The way forward appears to be within our scopes when enquiring how we must take into account how isolated we can become in searching for this hidden agenda. Many have tried finding it difficulty to sit in the silence for any length of time, this is natural to the normal mind shutting down the sequence of thought, when we can slowly come to terms with this the way will open up and moments of peace and tranquillity appear on the scene, helping the mind to a just to the incoming energy, when this unique process develops there is an aura of awareness never before realised. Elevated feelings become apparent within the brain and the mind heightening the perception to a level whereby a stable platform appears bringing in new ideas never before known dreamed of the light within the head begins to glow indicating the presence of a spiritual teacher wanting to come through onto your field of play, as time goes by joining of forces and mind becomes imminent this is through the desire to communicate with your spiritual doorkeeper. Who as been around you for many years decides that the time is right for you to join forces and you become an highway whereby inspiration is given to you for the benefit of your fellowman. You have sown the seeds in your mind and now you will watch then take root. The wise man is one who knows where he as been and knows where he is going he goes not dwell on mistakes but in all ernest attempts to rectify then one by one in order to purify his lower self through self analysis, this he can do he as the indication to change the pattern emerging within his mind with his will power, he then realise his strengths and weaknesses. By this time there is a significant awareness developing and gaining momentum, all this provides a deeper understanding within the structure of the cells of the brain you may say what as this got to do with the afterlife, well I have tried to give you in psychological terminology a way forward into the depths of the soul we keep on hearing the logical steps to be taken to arrive at the entrance to the aquatic records where all information is stored from the beginning of time , only a few are allowed to enter. They first must enter the hall of learning to embrace the seven seals of dawning of know time before enquiring the way to different planes of existence in cosmos. A similar pattern emerges when the spirit vacates the body and then becomes spiritually orientated entering its own sphere never before seen or envisaged there is no beginning and no end to the man upon this plane who as lined is mind soul and brain he realises his vocation in life is to follow his instincts appearing on the threshold of his mind his interest in the power surging through his veins is not just blood but the life force, this force then penetrates all living cells within the material body. The soul plays no part in this exercise all that is of material rots and decays in mothers earth. why then should I mention these physical attributes when dealing with the soul the most interesting aspects are in the body and mind relationship conceivable and most interesting the soul on its own plane is attractive energy magnetic drawn towards similar likes or dislikes in nature. today we realise change comes about regardless of who we are what we are what particular we may be on we have the ability to transcend beyond time and space tuning ideologies and set ways we have settled into on journey searching for the meaning of life after death we take it for granted that there is only one life upon this planet called earth and we are the sum total of previous lives we have lived it as been suggested we are a multi - dimensional entity surrounded by energy fields we live and have our being in this sea of force. Everyone as this intuition laying dormant until activated through certain opening of the psychic channels opening the door of perception. The impossible becomes the possible and the mind becomes expanded tapping into new avenues of knowledge adlibly the man then can pass on information to his fellowman the thoughts appear within the mind waiting to be expressed this stage is where the person may doubt this information arriving in his field of consciousness and may feel insecure this comes through practice. When the mind begins to realise the significance of the power it holds when under control, a feeling of security comes into existence, an independence at first bringing into manifestation past memories from the collective unconscious, to the conscious mind the person can recall these events automatically in detail. The big question is where is all these memories stored without getting mixed up. I have decided not to go to far into the mechanisms of the brain with all its highly sophisticated pathways there are specialist in this field who have mapped out where brain functions begin their course of action the psychological arguments for the student of metaphysical school vary in their approach this accounts for the many divisions in this field of enquiry so much can be learnt when we start to ask questions providing the interest is a valid concept which will add to our information mind. Describing the many pitfalls surrounding this illusive pathway describing the positive assumptions. When you have reached this stage of you journey into the unknown you become more conversant in the are of communicating with those who are around you in the ether, there are those who dedicate themselves to giving and passing on knowledge to improve the state of the world then there are those who become familiar guides who are most concerned with giving prove of life after death people ask the question why can't I communicate with my loved one's the answer is plain enough you have not got your psychic channels opened and you must remember we are dealing with a higher plane of existence beyond the normal mind. They cannot break through the psychic veil within the mind and brain. We are talking and dealing in the abstract subtle energy coming and penetrating the very core of our being. sometimes without being aware, we do get precognitive ideas momentarily, but as I have said the information coming through is rejected as been imagination through perseverance and believing this negative attitude will eventually disappear and stability will be order of the day. I have now come to the end of this manuscript hoping by now it may be of help to those seeking guidance in their lives. A relief appears to have lessoned my baggage which I have been carrying about for many years as though I have found a way of expressing my inner thoughts on paper. This manuscript as given me and encouraged me to feel more secure in my life becoming positive and more understanding towards others. This as come about through trial and error being good listener at times when confronted with obstacles created by negative thoughts. through this self analysis striving towards perfection learning each day can be better if you believe. Even when all seems lost, a fire burning deep within you appears on the scene motivating and directing you through all adversity. I do feel what as been written can be of benefit if taken in small doses, but if not no harm done. People may I see the world through coloured spectacles I wish that was true, we all have our cross to bear and we know that some have more disadvantages than others in this world. you will presume have noticed I do not mention the thing that makes the world go round, the word love it is very difficult to express this wonderful word, but may have hit some notes opening up melodies creating harmony and peace. Awakening the soul deep within you to enrich the material world on your journey into the world beyond be one with peace.

*Matthew Wilson*

# *The higher faculty called mind*

What is mind how can we establish a working hypothesis concerning this eternal continuous mysterious concept we partake every moment of our individual lives in this structure is of abstract nature and is none existence until given access by the interchanging of thought processes which become words acting on material substance when identifying and relating to the external world thousands of thought process never get to stage of words owing to then becoming aborted selectivity precedes this unique process subconsciously deeply embedded but as its own interrelating elements. so how can we describe in words, words that have little meaning we take for granted that which is presented to us as been valid and truthful without verifying its contents. This is one of the dilemmas we have to take into account in our everyday activity a person with an analytical mind analysis within his brain and then desyphons the meaning to be expressed in normal everyday speech. The secret behind this illusive concept will open up a vista of information never before recognised giving a broader sense of individualisation once the attraction through visualisation and imagination, the two key elements needed for the mind to recognise the ability following the most advanced information coming through adlib. You are intricate mechanism on this planet earth. No other species has the ability to change and transform the things around him, he as the capacity to alter anything that is presented to him in his life. Because he knows the laws of attraction.

Though this mode of expression he can also when required give a very good advise to his fellowman. what is the purpose behind all this, according to the teachings in metaphysical documentaries, we are evolving towards perfection in this cosmic jungle, maybe this is why there are differences between human being all on different levels of evolution that give us the probable of distinghsion do we know the cause of effect and the many misunderstanding it cause throughout our earthly lives or is there some other answer to this problem when we scrutinise in - depth the reason why we alter our minds instantly for better or worse, someday we may have the answer to describe the indescribable to become acquainted with the none familiar after continuous effort searching for the intricate methods the mind in all its resistance can at times rise above the petty arrogance and nonsensical attributes it as encounter over the years, the revelations and intuitive thoughts become an attractive force to be reckoned with on our stupendous journey we have taken on our path to enlightenment and at this stage things begin to happen after many years of manipulation , the mind develops an intriquite way of dealing with the rubbish that as accumulated within this all pervading entity. Sorting the wheat out from the chaff, there are many modes of expressive thought developing within the active mind at this stage the stillness of water overflowing with reasurrence now help the inner mind or lower one if you prefer this way of describing it with an abundance of solidifying substance as you my now say all the above is just rhetoric and maybe meaningless to many, therefore read dijest and recall that which maybe of benefit to you at this particular time. There is so much I can give and there is so much you can take aboard. I feel I have now taken a modest methodical approach giving you various constructive ways and means of analysing the essence and nature of the world beyond.

There are many roads to be taken before a man starts to look for his inner god, this comes through sheer methods of approach, he has enquired through self discipline and eventually excepted the way forward is to go within himself to find the knowledge and wisdom laying dormant his soul, this unique experience becomes a discovery into and beyond the physical domain, once he has felt this all pervading energy he becomes a beacon of light to other souls on this journey into the unknown. he stars to realise he is not just a body made of material substance and then a change takes place after many trail and tribulations searching for this golden thread uniting the spiritual with the physical, his journey as just began and he will achieve a certain amount of satisfaction in the process eliminating negative thoughts which he as been surrounded with. In the good book we are told that man will be born again, but not in flesh but spirit. Besides this illuminating experience his whole life changes, he then can see and hear the incoming messages from spirit. Guiding and directing his thoughts onto another plane of existence. His participation in his attitude and way of life he has concurred the ability to rise above situations that are detrimental to his way of thinking now.

It now appears to me that some people know just how to achieve the things they want in their lives, while other wish they could this is again knowing how to set your stall out. There are those who just sit back and say maybe one day I will achieve the good things in life and are still waiting for it to happen. Then there are the go setters, they know what they want and draw to themselves. This is fact and one of the reason comes about through the power of visualization, seeing with the mind eye and then projecting into the ether. Using the imagination to achieve the results they require. This again as to do with the person ability to concentrate and meditate on what they want to receive, there is an old saying, you must put something into get something out, nothing ventured nothing gained. In reality the magic is already there just waiting for the right time and the right place to manifest, what happens is you send the thought out into the ether by the power of the will which will then attract similar conditions, instead of just sitting back and hoping things will happen but they never do. we can change our ways of life if we are prepared to put some effort behind our thoughts, it is by thought we are destined to be or not, the answer is within your grasp, some people say you cant change the way you were born, but there is away you can, by being and really wanting the change to take place.

There are souls coming into manifestation and those entering the after life, this process is continuous cycle for each human being upon this planet earth. Some people ask the question is there more coming in than going out, I don't have the answer to that point put to me, statistics may argue on this assumption, but I believe it balances out eventually. According to the time and state of society not forgetting those who were taken through wars. Unnecessarily having now realised the soul when released from the material body functions on a different plane and vibrates beyond the 5 physical. each human being as a built in clock metaphorically speaking and when the ticking of this concept fails to tick in harmony with the corresponding body, death is imminent and the soul is released from its habitat. To watch person pass over is wonderful especially if you have the clairvoyant vision the majority of people are released through the head centre and stream of aluminous vapour can be seen momentarily I have witnessed this transition on many occasions having worked in a hospital seeing this with my own eyes, it is very hard to describe in words this feeling of elation proving once again the spirit lives on. it is not everyone's cup of tea to witness an event like this the next step is where does the eternal spirit go after leaving the material body in actual fact it arises and ascends to the plane that's as been prepared by your own hand while on the earth plane.

We have discussed briefly the all pervading powerful connection between the faculties we use everyday and the 7 sense. There are many diversities surrounding this phenomena, knowing certain criteria releases a small amount of energy without disturbing the structure and channel in our daily activities, when this is achieved there is a deeper understanding now apparent in your daily life. This is the beginning of new venture concerning the reliability once this commitment is apparent you may now say what does this entail to ordinary person what benefit will he derive from all this, firstly he becomes aware of his true self, and knows the difference between his lower self and higher self, there is only a very small degree to begin with but as time goes by the gap widens, so that the energy can pass uninterrupted through into his conscious mind you will also find problem solving a lot easer from now on life is so complicated to the ordinary man, by recognising this his life will change for the better.

# The psychic nurse out of this world written by Matthew Wilson

The purpose of this book is not to teach psychiatry, but to enlighten the ordinary person in the street regarding the everyday activities working in a psychiatric hospital. Nursing the many types of mental illnesses that confronts society in a modern setting. also the story of one particular man, forced with knowledge that he also could see and hear voices which he has to subdue on many occasions, while looking after the mentally sick having the gift of second sight and at the same time working under duress at time, knowing that the mind can and dose play tricks with humanity. The aim of this book is to bring across the many pitfalls and if possible show that we are all human and these conditions can appear and happen to the best of people. So I say to you all don't be to hasty in your attitude towards those afflicted as they belong to some ones mother. in my quest to do what I can in this field in my endeavour to bring a little happiness to those who for many reasons are suffering I say to you think before you speak. Hoping you may derive something from my experiences working in a psychiatric hospital. written by Matthew Wilson The following is a true story, an account of working in a psychiatric hospital looking after the mentally sick and the disturbed mind. One of the reasons I decided to take up this profession was because I was in forces in Korea in 1950 - attached to the 26'th field ambulance looking after the wounded and injured so I had some knowledge in the medical field so to speak. I got demobbed in 53, and then I had numerous jobs from that moment on until the years 1967 I applied for a student nurses post. I went for the interview and sat a test, they said we will be in touch with you in the next 2 weeks sending you a letter by post, ok I said I don't know whether I am putting the cart before the horse ? So I will tell you that after coming out the forces I met a nice girl who is my wife now, we have 4 children and many grandkids and great one's as well. So I have mentioned that as you mat think well his he or isn't he married or not. I was waiting for the outcome of my interview and the answer whether I had been excepted as the hospital to my surprise I received a letter confirming that I had been excepted and would I confirm this letter to them and the starting date I was in between jobs so it didn't matter about giving any notice in.

In the letter they sent me it stated for me to go to the main office on arrival, by the way the hospital was at least 9 miles from where I lived, so it was a bus ride there. When I got there I went up a long drive to the main offices and on top of the office was a big clock I found the place and was shown into the waiting room where others sat. I presumed waiting to be called regarding the position. so my turn came and was shown into another room, and sat at a desk was two people a man and a woman. The main introduced himself by saying he was the chief male nurses and the lady said she was the matron, and your name he asked, I told him my name and he said sit down, we pleased for you to join us according to your experience you have some knowledge in the medical field which will be helpful in your training. We have decided for you to train as a r-m-m registered mental nurses. It is a three year course consisting of anatomy physiology psychology and psychiatry you will be in the hospital teaching establishment 3 days a week to begin with we welcome you aboard and the shock hands just wait outside then we will show you and take you around the hospital. this he did and showed us different departments first of all and the proceeded to the wards I was not afraid at all been in the army so nothing came as a shock to me, just that I feeling sorry at sight of some of those poor souls, who I knew could not help or do anything about their condition. I just felt uneasy with others with me as I think some of them had not seen people like this before so the story goes. I started my nurses career and did shift work mainly, my weekly wage in them days was around 8.00 per week, no travelling expenses. When I was not at school, I did morning shift and then late ones starting at 2pm on the late shift Saturday night and change over early morning Sunday.

I was first working on a psycho - geriatric ward, and the charge nurses said to me, well lad how are you going to get here in the morning for 6am, as a rule the students have to sleep in the bathroom on mattresses, I said no way am I going to do that while I have a bed at home, but that put me in a dilemma you could say. so what was I to do under the circumstances, then it hit me working on the ward was a nurses who said earlier that he came my neck of the woods, so I asked him if he could do me a favour just this once, and he replied for Saturday night Sunday that. From now on I needed transport for Saturday night Sunday change over, through the week I went by bus what came into my mind was the week coming, I had to find some transport to me there. so I borrowed some cash of my mother and told her what it was for, I was alright has I had a past my driving test, also I drove awhile in the army a stretcher jeep. So the next week I bought a small car which was very helpful in those days. nursing on the geriatric ward was very hard work you could say, but very interesting getting to know the patients by name, and their conditions. Which help me when I went to school not all were very old some suffering from pre-senile dementia and some with psycho-physical disorders. most needed washing and shaving and bathing as some were double incontinent, to do all this before breakfast came up to the wards from the kitchens, most had to be fed and made sure that the breakfast was reasonably cut up into small portions. owing to some having difficulty in swallowing but not only that would not eat themselves, so it was a full time job.

In those days there were at least 60 patients on this ward and only 3 or 4 staff to look after them. My duties as a student nurses was to do the above while I was on that ward for a least 3 months of my training. As time went by I got more proficient in my nursing career. At the end of my shift I was ready for home my wife use to say are you sure you like doing that type of work? Has long you can mange on the pay I bring home , but it will pay dividends eventually as time goes by, and when I pass my exams. I did stint on the psycho - geriatric ward and then I was allocated to an admission ward, which was quite the opposite and was very interesting. The patients were mobile and could look after their everyday washing and dressing themselves. The admission ward was very intriguing, this was because you saw and came in contact with all different types of psychiatric conditions. Taking the patients history and background gave you some insight to condition they were displaying. The Drs would px medication if needed to help with the patients in their dilemma, it was very interesting to learn about the brain and its functions and what can go wrong with the cognitive and higher functions - also the mysterious mind - fascinating to understand these concepts before your very eyes. I spent 3 months on different types of wards gaining more experience has I went along. In school I learnt the different types of disorder and the classification, and also what types of medication to administer if and when required. You may now wonder what the title of story means, has I have not mentioned yes my abilities to see and hear beyond the five physical senses working in a psychiatric hospital having the gift of second sight gave me better insight in to the patients conditions. I had to be very discreet and you can imagine me wearing a white coat as well, but it also confirmed to me that my gift was genuine as I could prove what I saw and heard to be authentic not a

Delusion or an illusion, so there I was with my ability to see and know beyond the normal conditions. But as time went on some how it came about that I had this second sight and given prove to some of the nurses became a fascination and spread like wild fire. All though my training I was classed as the nurses with the expanded consciousness, but I knew when to keep quite and keep my mouth shut as there were nurses who did not believe in extra sensory perception, and there were those who understood this ability and asked me many questions about its validity. After the first year we had the hospital exam on what we had been taught in that year, and also a written paper which I passed no problem. Only a couple of years to go before I qualified and become registered. Time was passing by now it didn't seem that long since I stared my training learning about all different classification of mental dysfunction became more fascinating knowing what patient was suffering from and the Drs prescribing the to alleviate the symptoms gave one a sense of achievement. They say time is a healer, plus rest and recuperations and rehabilitations to send the patient back into society if possible that was the aim to do this and see it happened gave me great satisfaction. One of the problems I was faced with at times was when the nurses asked me to predict whether they would pass their final exam this was a dilemma for me as I did not want to say yes knowing for a fact it would be no. So I said to them who were going to pass yes and those who I saw fail I would say you have a good chance like everyone else I did not want them to dwell to much on it as it could alter their attitude. Having a wife and family I supposed help a lot I used to think about nurses in residents. You could say they were still on the premises and on the job, like anything else I had switch off not taking my professional work home with me. We were taught this by the teachers in the hospital school to separate the two if possible. There was still a lot of studying to be done I know I said don't take your work home with you I meant what was happening back at hospital, but of course had to take home from school the lessons to be studied I knew in my heart and soul this was my vacation and I felt a lot better for knowing this, it is surprising what can come about when you open your mind to higher knowledge I suppose in reality I had to do this somehow to be of service to other human beings who needed extra help in their lives. This story has not yet began properly yet as they is so much to tell you. You may laugh at some of the things and also cry which I suppose is only been human time was passing by and getting nearer to time for the big examination to become a r-m nurse. So it came the day of reckoning, three hours of writing everyone was a little apprehensive, hoping they would get some questions they were conversant with over the tree year. it seemed like a week sat there answering the written questions, then a voice from the heavens said stop I had cramp in my hand and both my legs so I was relieved to know this. I had just completed the paper and I felt a little apprehensive in the process. So that was that nothing more to be done only now to relax and go for a pint which I did. Then it was back to the wards as usual, some of the better patients ask me how did I fare with the exam I said hope I did ok and thanked them for there concern we were told that we would get to know our fate within a month from now, so best thing was to put it out of my mind and wait and see what the result was? By this time I was given the opportunity to take charge of a ward to gain experiences and to write out reports, this appeared to be normal which really was good thing thrown in at the deep end. That month seamed like a year and then it finally arrived from

The g-n-c general nursing council. I opened the letter and to my surprise it stated that you have passed the necessarily 3 years training and now you can call yourself a r-m-n and your name will be added to the register. I was delighted and excited and so was my wife who has stood by me for three years scraping pennies together as best she could, then I had to pay to become registered. By this time I was known by many patients and staff a like on different wards when I met them in the long corridors painted white and green I would not say it was good colour scheme? Most of the patients were allowed to wonder up and down the corridors, most of the wards had a number ranging from 1 to 20 so if you asked any patient walking down the corridor what ward were they from they could tell you. It was a community self sufficient with a lot of ground. I was sent for by the chief male nurse. And he was delighted at my progress and said that he was considering giving me the title of staff / nurse in those days. He was classed as a god, what he said went without question. So I received a pat on the back and became a staff / nurse which included more salary. By this time I was in the position to admit patients referred by clinics and Gps and those who were sent from the courts on a section, also most came in voluntarily as well but some came in on a section for observation. I believe now that the admissions and sections have been amended from the time I was nursing the time went by and we had turn over of patients some regulars and new faces and the long stay one's, you had to be a brother dad and besides being a nurse a counsellor to the patients who relied on your expertise you became like a big family sharing their needs and worries. By this time I was conversant with medical terminology about the different classifications of mental illness. I became more aware of patients conditions and the many

Changes can take place within the mind. It was nice to see patients discharged back into their own environment, this gave me a healthy satisfaction to see this and also been part of the recovery team. On one particular ward I was surprised when a patient said to me that I saw things and I said what makes you say that, he replied to me and said his mother in the spiritual world told him this and said that you are a good medium I didn't no whether to laugh or cry, because he telling the truth, so I said to him how long as your mother been telling you these things since she past over ten years ago but I don't often tell people things like that as they would say I was crackers so what could I say to him without offending him. Well I said your mother may be right so I did not pursue it any further, but it made me think. that there is only an hairs breath between insanity and normality you have only got to read the good book and it tells you of prophets long ago who knew and sensed these impressions so it was nothing new to me at all. You see my mother had a gift so you could say it was inherited if that is the right definition anyhow I kept it under my hat what he said to me, but knew he was right. I suppose these things come to try us in a roundabout way at the particular time who really knows the answer? Never a dull moment did I experience while working on the wards whether is was a long stay or admission ward or geriatric. They all needed attention one way or another, to be lost in your mind can be a terrible affliction to say the least. What shall I tell you now that may make you laugh as when you mention you work in a psyche hospital some people shudder with fear I think the public should become more aware and know that one out of 5 people can be afflicted with some form of mental distress so people in green houses should not throw stone's, as it has been written.

There were times when we had a laugh and sometimes it could be sad. The whole idea was to admit to treat and discharge when it was possible to do so nothing better when you see some one who came in so mixed up and then eventually went home, these were the good times for me, my next port of call was for me to do night shift which didn't bother me the least bit as some nurse were unsettled about ding nights and it has been said that some patients who had passed over were still walking the corridors as ghosts so I was in that unique position of been able to see them been as I was. Also given the job of taking the poor souls down to the morgue. So I was given the name remover I began to do nights taking over from the afternoon shift most of the patients were the same only it was night time and I knew which patient were insomniacs so I was already clued up in that quarter, the ward was the psycho geriatric one so there were two nurses in attendance as the majority were double incontinent and needed changing ever so often. The nurse working with me was a third year student who had volunteered to do nights I said to him you are not afraid, he said no not at all working with you as they say you know all about ghosts and such like . Do not believe everything you hear about me but I did tell him that I was sensitive which sounded better. We got on like an house on fire, we went round the known ones who were likely to be incontinent and change them. It was then just a matter of observing and quietening the noisy ones down we did four nights then we had three off it was a matter of getting use to the change over from days. I completed six month on night patrol as I called it most nights was the same nothing unusual to report only that I saw many apparitions who were harmless just like ones through the day. My next port of call was for me to work on a refractory ward

There were times when we had a laugh and sometimes it could be sad. The whole idea was to admit to treat and discharge when it was possible to do so nothing better when you see some one who came in so mixed up and then eventually went home, these were the good times for me, my next port of call was for me to do night shift which didn't bother me the least bit as some nurse were unsettled about ding nights and it has been said that some patients who had passed over were still walking the corridors as ghosts so I was in that unique position of been able to see them been as I was. Also given the job of taking the poor souls down to the morgue. So I was given the name remover I began to do nights taking over from the afternoon shift most of the patients were the same only it was night time and I knew which patient were insomniacs so I was already clued up in that quarter, the ward was the psycho geriatric one so there were two nurses in attendance as the majority were double incontinent and needed changing ever so often. The nurse working with me was a third year student who had volunteered to do nights I said to him you are not afraid, he said no not at all working with you as they say you know all about ghosts and such like . Do not believe everything you hear about me but I did tell him that I was sensitive which sounded better. We got on like an house on fire, we went round the known ones who were likely to be incontinent and change them.

On days. It was a semi closed ward as most of the patients had an history of aggression and disturb behaviour. Some were put there when they caused problems on other wards but also was sent by courts awaiting trail now then this ward was a different ball game, as I mentioned that the majority had a background of violent behaviour. And were severely disturbed and needed medication to calm their abnormal behaviour when required. This was a ward that required many staff consisting of a charge nurse two staff nurses and two to three students nurses at one time. To relieve the tension a qualified nurse who had trained in occupational therapy was allocated to the ward to try and show some of them things they could to occupy her minds, also a student nurse accompanied with a staff nurse would take a few patients off the ward round the grounds each morning and afternoon. Many times one would make off and we had to call in the local police to let them know one had got away. Some people asked me was it like the film one flew over the cuckoos nest. Similar characteristics I told them, but was real not make believe I told them they could visit on opening days to see and find out what was really going on for themselves. Anyhow this was the ward were thing just happened out of the blue, one instance on the late shift we were playing dominoes with few patients having good game, when I felt something was wrong and something was going to happen, my sixth sense was telling me this, but I did not realise what, until a patient standing close by made a sudden grab for the dominoes and started to swallow them, this happened so quickly we had no chance to stop him, but the beauty was he said what are you going to now and laughed. Well the only thing we could was to get in touch with consultant. Who came to the ward and said will send him for an x ray to see how they have lodged so this was the dilemma the patient was escorted to the nearest casualty department

With two staff. The dr then said the only thing we can do now is let nature take its course. Meeting that to give the patient a kidney dish every morning to see what he would pass and show the staff what was passed. The patient arrived back on the ward and the nursing staff that went with him was told he had several dominoes in his gullet and suggested what his doctor said. The patient acted as though nothing had taken place just laughed at the whole thing. So the procedure was told to him and he nodded. the next morning the patient came to the nurses office with the kidney dish full of excrement, was told to go back and wash the contents which he did, this continued each morning, some mornings he past two until he past no more so we counted seven in all. this particular morning the charge / nurse made out the ward report and would you believe it he put at the side of the patients name nothing seen must be knocking. Well this cause an uproar as the chief male nurse wanted to see the nurse in charge that particular morning, has he receives all the ward reports I can say that I had nothing to do with that comment. It appeared to be a standing joke but not in the eyes of c-m-n in the end he only got a verbal warning. now verification regarding classification of type of mental illness. Frustration - aggression hypothesis - aggressive behaviour is always linked with antecedent frustration, and that frustration always gives rises to come form of aggression. In the case of trauma to the head i.e left sided temporal damage, a person is unable to express himself verbally unable to swallow - unable to correlate frustration, this dose not mean the person is mentally ill. He still has feelings and thoughts, but is unable to construct them, thus turning the frustration into psychical aggression. This does not mean that the

person should be treated with major tranquilizers organic brain syndromes this encompasses a wide range and variety of conditions - bizarre behaviour resulting from specific traumatic injuries to parts of the brain, severe impairment of mental functioning impairment of language - perception, and memory processes, as well as emotional dysfunction. types of mental disorders psychiatric classification (1) hypochondrias is (2) depression (3) hysteria (4) psychopathic deviate (5) masculinity feminity (6) paranoia (7) psychathenia (8) schizophrenia (9) hypomania in those days some patients suffering from acute phases such as depression, also schizoid personalities were given e-c-t electric - convulsive - therapy - with their consent or the next of kin. I was not in a position to say whether it works or not but I can say that in some cases it showed good results. working on a refractory ward amongst a wide variety of patients with different conditions gave the students nurses a wealth of information in their plight to become r-m-ns you had to be alert most of the time and be ready if and when some one blew their top. This happened regular some patients listening to voices telling them what to do. A lot of them were suffering from auditory hallucinations and some visual we had what you call a full house, comprising of the following -

Psychopathic personality disorders - manic - depressives - paranoid schizophrenics - obsessive - compulsive disorders just to name a few, so has I said a mixture of many disorders. On one ward. It was good ward to learn your psychiatric disorders. Each patient was prescribed medication for their particular condition. At the bottom of the ward was 3 locked cubicle, these were only used in a emergency when patients needed to be segregated for there own safety as well as others. This was only use with the consultants permission as a calming down period, and for safety reason only. At times you can imagine how I felt having this perception and knowing what was going through their minds, very disturbing to say the least; I had to close my third eye which is centrally placed between the eyebrows. You could say that I was switching off. A patient came up to me he said can you see this person standing besides me, and he says you also can you see him, I said by the way who his he my granddad he replied he is wearing a flat cap and has scarf around his neck, I then said dose he speak to you often your granddad he replied yes most of the time, what does he tell you to do? He tells me good things not bad, we have a joke now and the he likes to cheer me up I had to tell you this has he said mention it to the nurse. These are just a few incidents that occurred while working on the wards. Another instance a patient said to me that he could see a lady around me very petite and she says her name is Martha I new who she was is was my grandmother on my moms side, so you see these things appeared spontaneously out of the blue what would the reader make of that? I am not trying to convince people as to its authenticity, but leaves room for thought. Another instance this patient said to me this will be the last time you see me, I wont be here tomorrow, I said don't talk like that I will see you tomorrow have a good nights sleep. I then left the ward and made my way home, I knew something was about to happen I had this nasty feeling all the way home. I returned to the ward the next day, to hear that the patient had choked on a humbug that lodged in his windpipe. I had a awful feeling in my gut. I was taken back with this, especially when I was told by the patient the night before and it took place, was it coincidence. I don't think so maybe he had this sense of leaving this world but not knowing how he would go, this baffled me, do we really know what is going to happen until it dose? Some answers are not forth coming nothing is straight forward in our lives? These mysteries open up a new concept to the minds of men. We can only at times get glimpses of things to come, where as the past is already written in the askasic records some where in the universe. But that is another story, as the poet said; there are more things in heaven than you can dream of. So where were we? Yes I was flabbergasted to hear this dreadful mews, but I kept it to myself under the circumstances these are things that stick in you mind another incident when I told a nurse to be careful going around a bend, as I see you having to break quickly, just a few words of guidance I said to be forewarned is to be forearmed and left it at that and though no more about it, until I heard that the car he was driving was a write off, but pleased to hear no one was injured. He made a remark like you wished that on me. I thought that was a insult, to be able to tell someone what is going to take place before it dose is a flash of inspiration to help the person concerned, I took no notice of what he suggested as I have met many people like that in the course of my travels. I was still nursing on this refractory ward, and on the certain day I was walking up the corridor and I heard a voice saying I told you so? I answered back and said what do you mean by that has I questioned some voices I had not heard before. It is me he went on to say, then I said who, well I told you you would not see me in the morning and now here I am.

A lump came into my throat then gave a giggle and said are enjoying your new life, he said yes no more pain no worry I am free to go where I want no restrictions I hope I have not upset you, not at all but am going on duty now and the voice disappeared. I felt better in myself knowing that he was ok in the afterlife I hope when people read this book don't think I am a nutcase far from it has I have read from prominent people over the years and many TV appearances also write ups in the national newspapers. So I though I would throw that in for good measure so here I was going against all the odds as much has to say if people saw me talking to deceased people they would want to lock me up and throw away the key. But my clairvoyance was the real thing and I had proved it time and time again over the years. It was only the doubting Thomas that did not understand this philosophy. when I went on duty I was told that two patients had decided to leave the ward when one of the porters opened the ward door and off like flash and not been seen since. I said to the nurses on the morning? Shift I have an idea where they will be, where you think the little café on the main road, I remarked so two nurses set off to the café in those days no such thing as a mobile phone within the half hour they were back on the ward as though nothing had taken place, that was a good guess one of the nurses said. Just a little bit of intuition and acted upon I said. Well the afternoon was very quite no problems to note, until one of the patients decided to swallow a spoon, here we go again so it was a trip to the casualty for an x ray has it happened they could just see the spoon at the back of his throat so they gave him a local anesthetic and removed the object.

Has you can see anything can take place when you have a ward full of patients who are very unpredictable, just sounds like a normal day. I think I was due for my days off and a holiday to boot so I put my application in for a fortnight starting the week after next I was ready for my break to be with family. on one occasion while taking a body to morgue on a trolley I felt a presence and to my surprise I saw the spirit of a man rising like smoke from around his head, it was beautiful to see this the smoke turned into many different colours I had never seen this before, it was a first time for me, inside the morgue the colours rose to about 2 feet above this physical body and then disappeared into thin air. This was something out of the ordinary when I found out he was a man of the cloth in his life time, I knew then he was no ordinary man as this showed itself to me, but proving this would be very difficult indeed. has long as I saw it and believed it was not a joke someone had done on me, I did not doubt for one moment its authenticity I felt a big relief knowing that this person had risen to his new abode very quickly. Leaving behind the physical overcoat. This made my day, where else was I able to witness and event like this. This was beyond words, cannot express such an episode. what next was I going to encounter in my nursing career this was beyond belief experience don't come everyday like that one so I will leave it to the reader to decide what I saw was real, as long as I know what I saw was genuine. Well the time came around for my holiday, and I was ready for it a fortnight to do nothing or anything I wanted to do. You see even when I was at home the phone would ring asking if I could give them a date and time for a reading. The wife said

Unplug the phone, you need a rest away from your inspirers so I took notice for once in my life and we had a quite restful 2 weeks doing hardly nothing. Nothing unto wards happened so it was back to work as usual I was greeted by staff and patients alike on my return. Had anything happened while I was on my 2 week leave. Nothing unusual I was told, only two different student nurse on the ward, nothing unusual about that as they were coming and going all time doing the rounds from one ward to the next. There was a note on the notice board for me to attend the day hospital for a week as the staff nurse had gone sick so would I deputise for him. I thought why me and then I thought why not it will be learning process for me has I had heard there were some unusual cases attending. I stared on the Monday morning not needing my white coat as it was informal dress at the day hospital I reported to the sister who I knew and I had worked on previous occasions so we had a good understanding. the sister said can I have a word in your ear, come into my office, it wont take long you know we have some unusual cases attending the d/h and I know you may be able to contribute to our team this morning we have a young male 17 years of age, who continues to wash his hand a compulsive hand washer, his diagnosis is obsessional compulsive disorder. Anyhow I would like you concentrate on his behaviour to see what you may come up with in the next couple of days we are want to try and get to the bottom of this appalling condition which he is effected with. So I will introduce you when he arrives I thought of you to deputise for a week knowing you background. So this youth arrived and the sister introduced me to him the first thing after that he said, I want to wash my hands is it ok you go and do that while I make a pot of tea, my first impression was that he had a guilt problem, and that something happened to him by someone to make him disgusted and to wash his hands to keep them clean, that was my first impression. He came back and sat down his hand were red and bleeding. I asked him was he alright, and he replied yes for the time being, I wont be a second will be back in a jiffy you will have notice by now that I have not mentioned ant names for certain reasons? So I will call this chap Holland I then went into the sisters office and told her what I had picked up psychically from him, yes you may be right at that, but he will not tell you, so don't ask him as he may go into his shell this was very intriguing some thing different bit this was not to be put in his notes at all. This was just my impression nothing substantial or fact, anyway we had a talk and he appeared to very intelligent and was interested in football and sport and knew quite a few things in that field, he appeared to open up more as time went by, but no mention of his condition. Deep down I got a the feeling he was soft at heart, and was kind in his approach I felt so sorry for him poor soul to be afflicted in this way. Has I said something deep down was eating him away and this causing the condition to surface into his conscious level of thinking which was interrupting his life. Taking on this bizarre affliction so that was my prognosis which was not official or fact but just my impression. The day came for him to undergo this test, and the consultant administered the drug into a vein slowly at intervals. He asked him are you feeling sleepy and the youth replied yes, then the Dr said I want you to tell me what is troubling you and why you have to wash your hands repeatedly. Take you time there is no hurry the Dr said so what can you tell me Holland well I don't know where to start I was sat on a park bench when this man sat down beside me and started to do awful things. I ran away and did not and could not tell anybody about this, and it was on my mind for a long time, the reason I wash my hand is to be clean again, the doctor then said from now on you will be alright now we have got to the root of your condition, have a sleep and you will be fine when you awake. the sister and I agreed with the Dr that Holland's condition was through this trauma he had with this dirty old man.

We did not mention our findings at all but we were on the right track so to speak. Holland recovered from his ordeal and never looked back; I was so impressed with how the consultant handled this case, very efficient indeed. I then was finished at the day hospital as the staff nurse was coming back the next day so I said my farewells to all the staff and patients and made my way back to main block. a good job done you could say, not all traumas are relinquished as fast as that one. That was a one off in my book when I got to ward the charge nurse said get yourself home will see you tomorrow. I did just that as he suggested, there are all memorise that keep coming back into my mind that is why I had to write this book. As you go along you can from your own opinion as to its authenticity, even if you don't you have heard and read what can take place in a psychiatric hospital there are people who care about mentally sick and devote their lives to looking after them god bless them who do and give then strength to carry on doing so. I will leave you now hoping you will have through all theses pages come to terms with the all the idiosyncrasy that we faced with everyday. written by Matthew Wilson r-m-n the end in year 2005

This book is about a short story that may look controversial at first, but after a few pages may make you think otherwise. Some of the things can and do happen in peoples lives, so therefore you can take it with a pinch of salt, on the other hand you may be able to identify with it. As many have had theses experiences in their lives, but at times to afraid to tell anyone in case they get laughed at. I have tried to make is sound reasonable at this point in time. So the reader can make their own minds up it is a story that can take place in some ones life. So you can make your own mind up, as to its validity? Take nothing for granted in this world of ours especially when you look around at what is happening in the world today with all the bloodshed and unhappiness that surrounds us. these are authors comments and remarks written by m-w the universal concept this universal concept arises within my mind more often than usual suggesting an attention to be recognised prior to it being isolated realising the mount of information given at any one time. This can represent at any given moment a duality syndrome effecting the very essence required to interpret the message from the brain system into moderate symbols activating consensus presumptions carried out within the framework of a neuronal explosion. once a neuron becomes activated it takes its course upon a certain line of least resistance and as to fulfill its stay of execution if a neuron fails to proceed it is terminated at source leaving the next impulse to germinate and fulfill its destination there is not one part of the body that does not respond at any given moment to stimuli throughout the millions of nerve endings there is also a built in system whereby the mind before hand can given a certain amount of information through the senses to be aware of external pain. I hope I have given you a certain amount of direction reasons a lot of people ask me why are we here what is the purpose if any, some ask is there any logic to it, and why are we like we are not to ourselves but to others. As in reality they see more of us than we do ourselves, when we start to enquire these possibilities a new avenue of thought emerges within the brain structure and questions from a higher cognitive approach begins to unfold in our makeup releasing specific energy fields from the inner most depths of the soul. Rectifying instant equations and sometimes leaving nothing to chance, considerably through following certain realistically methods their whole life now is centred on becoming more attuned to incoming vibration although this dose not happen straight away so therefore we do what we already know providing the sequence of events follow in the same direction. I think to myself at times was is the right thing to do, by saying what I said, I also believe in cause and effect and our responsibility towards others who may also be aspiring on the ladder to higher knowledge and wisdom In addition to this intensified moments whereby a special programmes concerning new advanced technology as been found to alter states of consciousness resulting in brain wave tales place is the introduction of sound or rhythmic beat to the auditory system causing a highly sophisticated awareness resulting in deep relaxation boosting the equilibrium achieved, removing stress factors. Producing high levels of endorphins and can alter other part of the brain system thus altering normal brain waves brining together a distribution of sound throughout the brain capacity when this is achieved a calmness and peaceful attitude develops and a sense of well been in everyday activity develops the left and right hemispheres become in harmony until the altered state of affairs ceases to be functional this is just a brief instruction when the mind becomes highly sophisticated through this concept. The union of the spirit within matter this comes into manifestation in association when the soul becomes infused in the interest of the lower personality on the lower level of the subconscious mind. Opening up new pathways leading to direct illumination uninterrupted identifying the valid within the realm of the cognitive ability to understand and comprehend a certain amount of detail balancing the quest within the framework of the existing duel system gathered from previous earthly existences of many life times my brain is still, the same and yet my mind cam become expanded with all the information passing through it reason and timing are crucial at any given time. Especially when new information to be digested. We now come to the part when we decide to makeup our mind and follow the great men of by gone days; this takes place more often than not. And many decisions will have to be consulted to be able from a working hypothesis the choice is yours to be considered. many attempts become possible in the process eventually eliminating many projects until the right approach proceeds to be beneficial in my book called the chronicles of a medium people appeared to be more interested in messages from the afterlife and the communication with their loved ones more than the philosophical attributes than mundane concepts, once again I feel obliged to mention spirit people while I am writing this book listening to what I am saying and writing this happens quite often, and in some instances want me to communicate with someone on the earth plane this can at times become a problem as their loved ones maybe hundred of miles away never before as the spirit in man become more apparent, people are believing and realising in this day and age we have improved our sense of awareness into the realms of this activity a new way of communicating is now required and new symbolic meaning that may open the psychic channels to be able to gross the rainbow bridge? Or build the anta carina to meet them half way the human mind is still in its infancy. Like its co - pilot the brain with all the millions of neural pathways.

The science of the human mind there are many

proposals when it comes to mind mechanisms one of the greatest mysteries ever told, whereby we realise this concept or not it still is one of the outstanding characteristics beyond our comprehension but what we do know is very limited in our approach to this vast subject we live and breath oxygen from the so called ether which surrounds and consumes everything known in the universe to man it is one of the elements which is free not man made the mind participates continuously in the energy field constantly brining and sending out information this then is a point I would now like mention concerning how a clairvoyant can receive information picking up thoughts within the bounds of probabilities from the etherise substances just mentioned, and this is how the magnetic attraction becomes a reality I have over the years through my gift and my spiritual guides tried to give my best in the process of helping people of all walks of life by my expertise into the subject people still ask that question, how do you know these things because there is that something within you need to be expressed verbal to other people who are searching for the communication between this earth plane and spiritual plane.

The melodic sound coming through the deepest part of my soul, gives me wonderful security and harmony in my everyday activity. To combat all negative thoughts instilled in my subconscious mind eliminating the none verbal sequences before entering my consciousness this whole sequence of affairs gives me a very good relationship and understanding into the mechanisms of the mind in all its secrets and mystifying considerations we have taken into account the different approaches when trying to establish a working hypothesis as to the relationship undertaken in unravelling the many principals involved. It is said the more we know the lese we are likely to comprehend when the time is right owing to a invisible screen covering the field of conscious and unconscious realms it is when this web like substance begins to open periodically we have glimpses into a new avenue of thought called intuition

The theme running throughout this book is concerned with the soul verses matter in manifestation, and the conceptual awareness while searching for valid answers to the world beyond, this then is my way of explaining the fundamental principals involved. Brining into focus certain aspects concerning the way forward gaining momentum every step of the way in the year 1990 I thought my time was up after having numerous heart attacks then under going triple coronary heart by pass. Then a voice in my head spoke to me and said your time is not up yet as you have a lot of work to do in this material world, brining the two worlds together when possible. That was 20 years ago. Now I suffer from Parkinson's disease plus gout-diabetes but these are only physical conditions the real person is not really effected as you know this to be a fact. Anyhow enough said about me. I will survive. To complete my work upon this earth plane. But like anything else nothing last for ever, only that dynamic pulsating concept which survives we call energy and spirit collecting knowledge and wisdom for future reference in this everlasting journey into the unknown

It as been suggested by many, when we pass over into the spiritual world all our worries and anxieties we no longer possess, the memories and experiences we went through in material body quickly dissolves and become records in the etheric chambers in the cosmos where all records are kept this is very intriguing to know this and we can at time consult the elders who have access to these records and are known as the masters of the words. The whole universal concept is nothing but abstract thought and is designed to order and maintain equilibrium, where as come across, this they do automatically because of no recognition given to them concerning life and the fundamental principals involved. When we can understand our very nature and what we are suppose to do while manifesting through a material body, for the majority have no idea of this wonderful thought provoking essence we call life. not until we have learnt many lessons can this concept be appreciated, and become a reality in our lives we are all susceptible at any given moment to in coming distractible thoughts also we must bear in mind we live and have our existence in this thought world

# I have been told

There are as many guides in the ether, some old ones some new ones waiting to communicate with those left behind on the earth plane to let them know that life continues beyond the physical plane of existence and reassure them by identifying themselves to the medium for recognition in some instances plane, name conditions dates are mentioned for recognition, the problem arises sometimes in the interpretation given by the spirit people to the mediums guide knowing these facts help everyone concerned in this art of communication. Some people have a common factor an hidden agenda built in to their nervous system which can alternate with mood swings, you may say what as that got to do with spirit communication, it is that concept which responds to higher vibrations at any given moment. The purifying of the etherise and astral bodies become more pronounced and the energy surrounding theses subtle bodies opens the gateway for the psychic faculty to develops enabling the person to progress further the spiritual kingdom as been mentioned time and time again as the world of thought, which continues after death.

# The 7 sense comes into play

When the third eye becomes active through continuous meditation over many years, the mystical 3 eye develops and becomes vibrant having access to the cosmic realms within the universe the eye covers all activity from birth to the passing of the physical body the collective awareness from being and individuality component to being with, enters from a dream state brining into focus the divine thread joining all and everything together, you may now wonder what I am talking about but believe me there is no fooling around when the right amount of knowledge is realised in the development of this subtle energy - at time there maybe a heighten and tingling sensation between the eyebrows, this is the energy passing through the psychic channel at that particular moment, I hope you don't think I have gone over the top by going on about certain aspect concerning the metaphysical eye. Now that we have established a certain and developed a working hypothesis into the remarkable working of the ultra mind. We may now put aside certain meaning relating to the spectrum where dwells the soul as we get older and the body starts to decline through wear and tear also the mind starts to play tricks with our everyday activities, we look back at the experiences we went through memories entering the mind sometimes brining joy laughter tears reminding us of these past episodes as though they conditioned in one way or another by these automatic responses in accordance with the so called kasha is where all these memories live. in esoteric psychology these elements remain a strong possibility where the seer or medium can have access at any given moment in time to those halls of knowledge and wisdom, nothing at anytime goes unforeseen, every thought word and action are kept in situ there are keepers whose responsibility is to guard the key to the doors where these manuscripts are stalled these entities are methodical in their approach. Their job is to have direct knowledge besides experience in the levels of human behaviour. Having direct insight into the depths of the inner mind of humans.

For the most part of our lives we are surrounded by invisible entities some higher ranking than others upon the ladder into the realms of spiritual awareness. Some people call them guardians of the thought processes among other things. Very difficult at times to distinguish between the lower entities and those who have direct connection with our etherise double. We dwell in the forever seas of interconnecting energies playing on our inner and outer sheaths giving our present situation some recognition and the ability to converse with our subconscious mind. When the mind becomes fragmentised through certain abnormalities from certain aspect the lower man transcends beyond the starting point on his long journey as time evolves and the continuing presence of these permanent entities become an established fact, the process begins to take shape. It as been suggested by many people the conditioning reflect action is a response to certain stimuli when repeated. Also the power of constructive visualisation brings into the equation a volume of ideologies which can be ilistrateted when the memory faculty becomes intact. there remains unidentified solutions in the presence when the mind starts to wonder and day dream in the waking state we all at some stage partake in this concept and by doing this we elevate the pressure within our brains and minds

# *When the soul becomes recognized*

This comes to fruition when the process is understood and recognised the principals involved begin to take shape do we realise the implications involved in proceeding along a given path whereby the soul on its own axis evolves through persistent gathering momentum gaining ground and becoming solidified. This entity recognises the pathway to be taken when the elimination of certain methods are applied how then can we describe this elusive invisible subtle energy what we can do is watch it develop and progress within the structure of matter while in a physical body, we cannot determine its progress out of the body as there is no time in the afterlife. Only the path to enlightenment. So what then is the descriptive analysis when trying to define this universal commodity. Each individual soul is the accumulation of experiences gathered over many years through darkness into the path of sheer brilliance lighting the way forward into infinity.

This section of the book will be to give the reader

more stories and messages from the world beyond as they were given to me by my guide white feather and my Chinese mentor. Who have been with me now for many years helping those who required guidance in their lives, the cheaper begins concerning a man who wanted his story to be told my name is John and I want to tell you a little of my life I wad a soldier in the 19 14 18 war just 17 and was called up to fulfil the king shilling in those days and was drafted to the front line in France. My elder brother was also in the forces, I felt behind my wife Alison who was two month pregnant, I remember the day we landed on the French soil under the barrage of shells and was hit by a bullet to my chest, I lay there some time wondering if I was alive soon or dead I soon found the answer to that question as I felt no pain and at the same time I was outside of my body looking down at if laying in pile the next thing I knew I was standing in the graveyard looking at my relatives who had turned out to see me put into mothers earth, you can imagine how I felt at all this, and I useless to do anything, no one could see or hear me, but I felt the sadness around the grave. I suppose this is one of many episodes that take place

As you know there are thousands of such stories that can be told you have only got to listen to the people here one minute and gone the next most people when past over want to tell their loved one there is continuity of life beyond the earth plane when we pass over into the world beyond. Living so many years on the earth plane not knowing that life continues regardless of whom you were in the material world. Everything in the process of decay and elimination made of matter, where as the soul cannot be destroyed and functioned on a higher frequency. gaining momentum each time when entering the physical plane. There is so much unexplained rhetoric and not may answers when question are put forwarding this area, when confronted very little is said on this subject, the majority of people remain sceptic and some would rather not know as this existence remain the only one to their consciousness? I suppose this entire field of endeavour will as time passes by becoming more open to suggestive thought the way forward is just beginning to become a open door whereby communication can pass from one plane of existence to another with ease and not complicated

I come to let you know the knowledge that has been given to you through my channel comes from higher order in the cosmos circle of life, so don't be afraid to open your hearts and minds to this level of consciousness, you may ask why this is reverent in this day and age, well first of all we need inspiration as never before, we have forgotten our true nature, but once we realise this many doors will open up to the one is sincere in his search which will eventually set you free from all adversities do not let negative influences take root, have no doubt and fear and try and set aside those setbacks you may encountered, these are impediments, the truth will set you free and show you the way forward. I now know my mother is at rest and is at peace where she is in the spirit world, I receive messages from her often, you may not believe what I am going to tell you about my dear mother, it will take some believing her work in the spirit world consists of being spiritual undertaker when a person passes over most of the time the person is not aware where they are sometimes called lost souls, and they float about between the two worlds, so my mother is one of the team whereby they do recovery work and help the through this transition.

We may now be a little closer to the path of enlightenment how close still remains to be seen, depending on the individual capacity to follow instructions to the letter, when applied with sufficient effort remarkable things start to happens change becomes a way of life, the new arrives within the spectrum opening a vista of never ending quality thrusting the soul into a world we can now understand with clarity this manuscript is and contain inspiration direct from the spirit world there is no beginning and no end to this realisation we call spirit the spirit is the character and designed concept to be given the thought pattern within the mind, once we verify this as a realistic pattern of events, there is no stopping the energy from taking precedence when understand you may say does this represent the whole essence and totality we are confronted with when searching for this mysterious phenomena. Words can only describe certain aspects of this illusive concept and negative summations can be detrimental within the mind if not guarded upon. so therefore thoughts of negative attitude can and does interfere with the channelling higher truths.

We may now be a little closer to the path of enlightenment how close still remains to be seen, depending on the individual capacity to follow instructions to the letter, when applied with sufficient effort remarkable things start to happens change becomes a way of life, the new arrives within the spectrum opening a vista of never ending quality thrusting the soul into a world we can now understand with clarity this manuscript is and contain inspiration direct from the spirit world there is no beginning and no end to this realisation we call spirit the spirit is the character and designed concept to be given the thought pattern within the mind, once we verify this as a realistic pattern of events, there is no stopping the energy from taking precedence when understand you may say does this represent the whole essence and totality we are confronted with when searching for this mysterious phenomena. Words can only describe certain aspects of this illusive concept and negative summations can be detrimental within the mind if not guarded upon. so therefore thoughts of negative attitude can and does interfere with the channelling higher truths.

I feel now I have in one sense tried to give the reader within my limitations a brief account regarding the fundamental principals reaching at times deep within my being for certain guidelines to following the path of enlightenment to bring those hidden revelations into the present moment so that you can continue your assignment to letter according to the progress you have achieved on your journey absorbing as much as realms whereby knowledge will be revealed. once again I can only give you certain aspects for you to deal with at any given time. It entirely up on you to decide the moment to install within your mind the characteristics you may develop hoping you have chosen the right approach when deciding when the time is within your capacity you have within the ability to restructure your thoughts according to the energy pulsating through your channels at any given moment you may feel you want to express yourself in a manner distinct from your normal self this is normal sequence of events

The idea is now to contemplate on the best possible way of obtaining the information that is in the subconscious mind without interfering with the know everyday activity and learned processes available at our finger tips we use constantly when communicating to one another the nest possible way of obtaining this result is by stilling the awareness holding the mind steady in the zero sense. Nothing coming in nothing going out, just the eternal now no yesterdays no to days or tomorrows just being through the silence everything is and will be pure senses? The longer the mind is in this state the stronger the effects become when in the normal state this may take years to develop but nothing goes unforeseen

The royal road to bliss can be strenuous playing havoc with a persons way of life, when he start step when commencing his journey giving up most of the things that as attached themselves whereby to him, these constitutes in time to a state whereby changes come to him when this realisation is imminent, what does this imply, it means we all can change in this process when adopted. when we apply a certain amount of energy purposefully the inevitable becomes a characteristic in our approach balancing the pair of opposites in a way that will start a line of least resistance directing a division o a temporary basis this in fact becomes away forward when realised on more ways than one you may now have to read the above more than once to benefit from what as been said so that you will become acquainted with this knowledge presented to you this the I will leave to your own digression

*Matthew Wilson*

# *Mind beyond time and space*

If there is anything beyond time? There appears o many discrepancies in the way we formulate ideas and concepts relating to this abstract phenomena many points come to the surface when enquiring the possibilities arriving within the activity of the brain then all of a sudden a spark of divine essence appears on the scene with a different solution making the way forward more accessible driving the elements in one direction this the starts at continuous path forward enlightenment the knower then becomes the knower in the field of knowing that which was out of sight becomes visible to the eye of the beholder in more ways then anticipated as time evolves within space the infinite sparks gets stronger resulting in a mind more active to coming energy the light in the head becomes more pronounced and becomes more stable and constructive from now on

# *In the mist of life we face death*

This is a fact, the question now rises for what purpose are we living this existence knowing full well there is a time to depart this earth plane, many reason come to mind to everyone no matter who they maybe, at times it don't make sense as to why we are born live die in that order, this appears to be a natural process of events somehow given to us to perform certain modes of expression to communicate within the bounds of all probabilities bringing together accumulative knowledge and awareness creating a stable continuity within the framework of existence having gain a certain amount of ideas and ideals the mind becomes the bearer of idiosyncrasies causing irritability and confusion at times we are all effected at sometime by these attitudes entering the mind realising outcome prior to having no know implications, we can take these attributes in our strides, and no be to effected by the outcome it presents individual concept brings into focus the realisation when the mind expresses certain amount of unknown ideas when confronted within ideologies connecting minds to certain modes of expressive requirements evolving the selective analytical approach to the scientific approach to the mind when the mind is in distractible attitude and aggessesion is in the pipe line, changes of behaviour creeps into a person attitude and assumes command by irritable thought sequences displaying negative responsiveness on the part of the response in the event of defining the right words to express within] the scale of 1 - 10 the buildings blocks remain the same when the mind tunes into the higher vibration giving rise to many individual concepts different expressions become apparent when enquiring the way forward the mind is the jewel in the crown in all its glorification I will leave this up to your digression

# *Controversy causes many disruptions*

When the mind cannot make a decision then there is doubt occurring within the selective pathways leading to the word maybe possible after taking into account the incoming energy waves enlightening the brain structure disturbing the balance of activity and a slowing down process begins to take place causing the following conditions lack of insight a slow progressive depreciation in the ability to communicate with your fellowman in a conversation this comes into effect when the brain through trauma slowing down of neurons through arterial disease thses changes come about making ones life meaningless and unable to continue with normal everyday activity he condition I am referring to is called dementia or alzheimer's decease the mind in a sense is out of time and space there is no cure for this condition it is slowly progressive there are many stages even pre-senile dementia

Now we come to personality traits and a diagnostic approach to this vast subject covering a wide range of psychiatric disorders and topics, it as been suggested that 5 out of 10 people will suffer some form mental illness in their lifetime, some will recover and some will better ate with mew medicines and new approaches in this field a persons life can be effected in more ways than anticipated all typed of mental illness can have their highs and lows depending on the person personality and will power plus the positive attitude ones as in communicating with everyday activities next is depressive illness, used to be called manic depressive psychosis, nowadays called bipolar- manly mood swings there is at the moment many articles written about this and medicines called lithium carbonate

I am 78 years old and have written a few books on the theme concerning the afterlife I find now how difficult it is writing this manuscript owing to my condition called Parkinson's disease also I am suffering from severe gout plus diabetes. in the year 1990 I underwent triple coronary bypass grafs. Which left me with pending heart failure. I have managed to keep my head above water, also have a son who was attested in the year 2001 left with brain damage, suffering from anoxic diffused cerebral damage. And needs 24/7 care my wife is also a very ill person suffering from myloma and recently had a back operation I hope that all this information will not put you off reading my book, which can be bought on the internet and ordered through leading book stores. Smiths-waterstones best wishes from matthew wilson

ND - #0261 - 080726 - C0 - 197/132/8 - PB - 9781844268917 - Gloss Lamination